A Tool for Letting Go of
Resentment *and* Anger

A Tool for Letting Go of Resentment and Anger

Short. Straightforward. Transformative.

A. Sehatti, RN, MSN
Family Nurse Practitioner

NCWC/Amend-Health Press

A TOOL FOR LETTING GO OF RESENTMENT AND ANGER: Short. Straightforward. Transformative. Copyright © 2022 and 2023 by A. Sehatti, RN, MSN, Family Nurse Practitioner.

All rights reserved.

No part of this book may be reproduced in whole or in part, translated, stored in a retrieval system, or transmitted, in any form or by any means such as recording, electronic, mechanical, microfilming, or otherwise, without the prior written permission of the author (A. Sehatti, RN, MSN, FNP) or NCWC/Amend-Health Press.

ISBN 978-0-578-29723-1 (paperback)

| Resentment | Anger | Relationships |
| Mental Health | Behavior change | Total Wellness |

Printed and bounded in the United States of America
First Printing: November 2022
Revised January 2023

Published by:
NCWC/Amend-Health Press
AKA Nutritional Counseling and Weight Control Clinic
51 E. Campbell Avenue, Suite 129 - 154
Campbell, CA 95008
United States
www.NCWC-AmendHealthPress.com
www.EatActThinkHealthy.com

"A Tool for Letting Go of Resentment and Anger" is a companion to "Accountability and Empowerment: A Four-Step Strategy for Overcoming Resentment."

Although it is recommended that readers work through both books to receive the maximum benefit, you can still gain a transformative experience by exploring either one independently of the other.

> *This workbook is not intended to be a substitute for counseling or the advice offered by a mental health professional.*

*Letting go of our feelings of resentment does not
mean accepting other people's hurtful behaviors;
Nor does it mean blaming ourselves for our feelings of
hurt, anger, frustration, disgust, hatred, or jealousy . . .*

*Rather, letting go of our feelings of resentment
is about genuinely releasing such feelings
so that we could emotionally detach ourselves
from those whom we resent:*

*For it is when we are emotionally free that
we can think clearly, see our choices, and
lead a proactive and fulfilling life.*

*Then, in essence, to let go of our feelings
of resentment is to retake our personal power
and control over our lives.*

*Let your feelings of resentment awaken and
mobilize you, not enslave you.*

About the Author

A. Sehatti is a registered nurse and family nurse practitioner. She received her bachelor's degree in nursing from University of Pennsylvania and her master's degree in nursing from UCLA.

Aside from her clinical work at such places as Stanford, UCLA, and Caltech Health Center, Ms. Sehatti has over forty years of experience in educating adults and children on total wellness. She currently works as a health educator and nutritional consultant at a private practice that she established in 2005 in Northern California.

A. Sehatti is highly dedicated to making a difference in people's lives. It has been the reward of witnessing people reach their health and wellness goals that has inspired her to write books and share the tools that have helped her clients with her readers.

Contents

About This Book		i
What Are Some of My Ways of Thinking, Feeling, and Behaving?		v
1	An Overview: Overcoming the Feelings of Resentment	1
	The Steps of the Self-Accountability Process	5
2	What Is Happening? What Do I feel?	9
3	I Feel Offended	13
	Empowering Self-Talks	29
	My Self-Talks	34
4	I Feel Annoyed	37
	Empowering Self-Talks	83
	My Self-Talks	86
5	I Feel Jealous	89
	Empowering Self-Talks	103
	My Self-Talks	107
6	I Feel That I Have Been Wronged	111
	Empowering Self-Talks	133
	My Self-Talks	138

About This Book

This book presents a unique and effective technique to help you let go of your feelings of resentment (i.e., anger, hurt, frustration, disappointment, bitterness, jealousy, disgust, rage, or hatred) and avoid the downward spiral that holding onto such feelings may create in your life (Page xix).

This strategy empowers you to become aware, find answers, resolve issues, and move on with your life when you experience stress in your relationships.

A Tool for Letting Go of Resentment and Anger contains self-inquiry questions; worksheets; inspirational words, quotes, and viewpoints; and, empowering scripts.

Through offering thought-provoking questions that you ask yourself as well as providing worksheets for writing down your answers, this transformative workbook helps you discover your true feelings and hidden thoughts during stressful times in your relationships: *Do I feel annoyed? Do I feel offended or do I think that I've been wronged? Do I feel bitter and resentful because I am comparing myself and thinking that I am less than the other person?*

The short inspirational viewpoints and quotes that are offered throughout this book are designed as such to trigger analytical and critical thinking and help you find answers and see choices.

Empowering scripts are provided to enable you to retake your personal power, resolve issues, and achieve a state of inner peace.

A Tool for Letting Go of Resentment and Anger uses a self-talk format to convey its message. This is to slow you down and help you become present and reflective—It is through the process of self-awareness and self-reflection that we gain access to our prefrontal cortex and become empowered to retake control, make better choices, and let go of our feelings of resentment in times of stress.

The first part of Chapter 1 briefly explains how the strategy used in this workbook helps you overcome your feelings of resentment. The second part of the chapter outlines the process for getting there and achieving this goal.

Chapter 2 helps you better understand what you are experiencing when you are stressed in a relationship with someone: It does so by asking you to identify the specific feeling that this unpleasant encounter generates in you: Do you feel *annoyed*? Do you feel *offended*? Do you feel *jealous*? Or, do you feel that you have been *wronged*?

When you identify your specific emotional experience (i.e., feel offended, annoyed, jealous, or wronged), you will be directed to the corresponding section (Chapter 3, 4, 5, or 6) that deals with the related experience.

About This Book

The self-inquiry questions presented in Chapters 3 through 6 trigger thoughts and help you become aware of your hidden thoughts and the root cause of your emotional state. This discovery is key to retaking your personal power and regaining your control.

The empowering scripts that are included in these four chapters enable you to find a sense of resolve and inner calmness.

At the end of each of these chapters (Chapters 3-6), a few pages are offered for you to craft your own self-talk scripts. It is the author's recommendation that readers design these dialogues in a manner in which they could revisit them during future stressful times—when you feel resentful and experience a sense of loss of control.

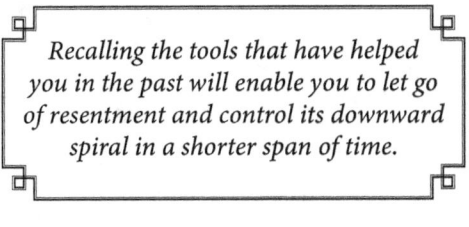

Recalling the tools that have helped you in the past will enable you to let go of resentment and control its downward spiral in a shorter span of time.

Before proceeding to Chapter 1, please take some time to reflect and ask yourself the thought-provoking questions on the next several pages. These questions are designed as such to get you started on your journey.

A Tool for Letting Go of Resentment and Anger

> *For further exploration of the root causes of resentment and ways of dealing with them refer to this book's companion, "<u>Accountability and Empowerment: A Four-Step Strategy for Overcoming Resentment</u>."*

What Are Some of My Ways of Thinking, Feeling, and Behaving?

1. Do I generally tend to *overfunction* in my relationships? In other words, do I commit myself to helping, taking care of, or fixing other people's problems even though they are capable of helping themselves?
   ☐ Yes   ☐ No

   If yes, then why do I do that?

If I have a tendency to overfunction in my relationships, then do I usually end up feeling resentful at some point in time?
☐ Yes   ☐ No

If yes, then what are some of my feelings and thoughts at such times that I experience resentment towards the people I overfunction for? For example, do I feel hurt, angry, used, or unappreciated? Do I think that I'm being taken for granted by them? Do I think that I am not important or that I don't matter to them?

_____
_____
_____
_____
_____
_____
_____
_____
_____
_____
_____
_____
_____
_____

2. Generally speaking, when people ask me about my feelings, opinions, thoughts, needs, desires, or hopes, do I communicate them freely, candidly, and straightforwardly?
   ☐ Yes   ☐ No

   If *no*, then why not? What keeps me from expressing myself?

   _____
   _____
   _____
   _____
   _____
   _____
   _____
   _____
   _____
   _____
   _____
   _____
   _____
   _____
   _____
   _____
   _____
   _____
   _____
   _____
   _____

3. In general, do I tend to spend a great deal of time replaying events and thinking about the interactions that I have had with others?
☐ Yes ☐ No

If yes, then why do I do that?

_____
_____
_____
_____
_____
_____
_____
_____
_____
_____
_____
_____
_____
_____
_____
_____
_____
_____
_____
_____
_____
_____
_____

4. Do I often find myself getting offended in my relationships?
☐ Yes ☐ No

If yes, then, generally speaking, what situations make me feel offended?

___

A Tool for Letting Go of Resentment and Anger

How do I usually deal with my feelings of resentment when I get offended?

What Are Some of My Ways of Thinking, Feeling, and Behaving?

5. Do I often find myself getting annoyed with others?
   ☐ Yes   ☐ No

   If yes, then what about others annoys me the most?

How do I usually deal with my feelings of frustration, irritability, or anger when I become annoyed?

6. Do I often find myself being jealous of other people?
   ☐ Yes ☐ No

   If yes, then what about others usually makes me become jealous of them?

   _____
   _____
   _____
   _____
   _____
   _____
   _____
   _____
   _____
   _____
   _____
   _____
   _____
   _____
   _____
   _____
   _____
   _____
   _____
   _____
   _____
   _____
   _____
   _____

How do I usually deal with my feelings of jealousy?

7. In my close relationships, do I *often* find myself feeling hurt and thinking that I was wronged?
   ☐ Yes   ☐ No

   If yes, then, what do I do in such times? How do I deal with my feelings of resentment (i.e., hurt, anger, rage, or hatred) when others cross my boundaries and violate my basic human rights?

A Tool for Letting Go of Resentment and Anger

8. Generally speaking, do I tend to hold onto my feelings of resentment?
   ☐ Yes   ☐ No

   If yes, then why?

A Tool for Letting Go of Resentment and Anger

If I typically hold onto my feelings of resentment (i.e., anger, hurt, frustration, disappointment, bitterness, jealousy, disgust, rage, or hatred then how has hanging onto such feelings has impacted my life?

What Are Some of My Ways of Thinking, Feeling, and Behaving?

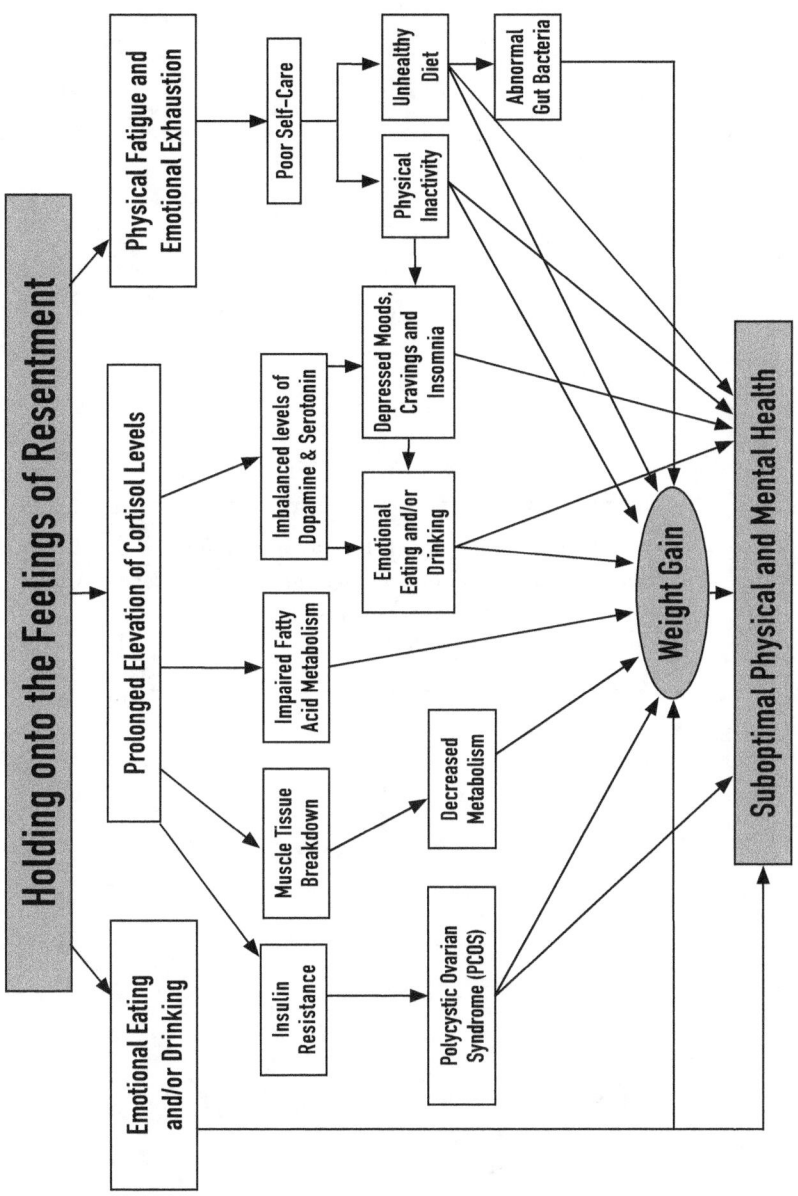

> "Holding on to anger is like grasping a hot coal with the intent of throwing it at someone else; You are the one who gets burned."
> —Buddha

> *When we remain unaware and live on autopilot, we may unwittingly live a life that leads to conflict, anger, and resentment.*
>
> *This is when the past gives meaning to the present.*

> *When we examine the past, learn from it, and become aware, then we live a life free of resentment.*
>
> *This is when the past stays in the past.*

> *Look at the rear view window only to move onward.*

9. What is one behavior that I would like to change or improve in myself?

1
An Overview: Overcoming the Feelings of Resentment

I am aware that I have little or no control over other people. Therefore, when I experience resentment towards others, I look inwardly, rather than outwardly, to regain my control and find inner peace.

When I look within and focus on myself, I arrive at valuable information: I become aware of my own *patterns of thinking* that drive my *actions* or *inactions* and lead to my emotional suffering.

I come to this knowledge when I engage in *introspection*:
When I *connect* with my *Self*;
Ask thought-provoking questions; and,
Reflect and make sense of all that I observe about my inner thoughts, self-talks, and way of being.

My self-discoveries empower me to see the big picture, find answers, and see choices (the Aha-Moment).

In such a state of self-awareness, I become empowered to stay in control and choose the course of action that results in rewarding outcomes.

As I resolve issues and let go of my feelings of resentment, I reach a state of inner calmness.

Chapter 1

This is how working through the process of *genuine accountability* empowers me to achieve a state of serenity, self-command, and tranquility (i.e., a state of equanimity) when I experience stress in my relationships.

An Overview

> "It is far more useful to be aware of a single shortcoming in ourselves than it is to be aware of a thousand shortcomings in someone else. For when the fault is our own, we are in a position to correct it." —Dalai Lama

Chapter 1

> *Self-accountability doesn't mean blaming ourselves; Nor does it mean that we justify or condone other people's poor treatment of us.*
>
> *When we hold ourselves accountable for our part in our conflicts or emotional experiences, we are only taking responsibility for the choices that we make (i.e., our actions or inactions).*
>
> *Source: <u>Accountability and Empowerment</u>: <u>A Four-Step Strategy for Overcoming Resentment</u>*

The Steps of the Self-Accountability Process

When I experience stress in a relationship
or in an interaction with someone, I embark on the
process of self-accountability to overcome my feelings
of resentment, gain inner peace, and move onward.

In the first step of this process,
I connect with my inner *Self* and become aware of
the feelings that this experience has generated in me.

I acknowledge and validate *all* of the emotions that
I feel (including such intense emotions as hatred).

I keep in mind that, as a human being,
I feel a wide range of emotions:

All human feelings are real, valid, and acceptable.

I understand that it is only when I become reactive
(i.e., act upon my negative emotions) that my feelings
become unhealthy and maladaptive.

This understanding mindset allows me
to *own* all my feelings of resentment without
being self-deprecating or self-critical.

Identifying, acknowledging, and validating my
feelings takes me to the next phase of my journey.

🌺 🌺 🌺

Chapter 1

In the second step of the process of self-accountability,
I ask myself: *"Why do I feel the way I do?"*

As I search deep down for an answer,
I become aware of the hidden thoughts and self-talks
that have generated my feelings of resentment.

This awareness takes me to the
next phase of my journey.

In the third step of the process of self-accountability,
I become reflective:

I examine my inner thoughts and self-talks and
understand how they have impacted my experience.

As I understand what happened and why I feel the
way I do, I come to see choices.

This discovery takes me to the
last phase of my journey.

In the final step of the self-accountability process,
I retake my personal power: I stay secure and strong
and deal with the issue in a non-reactive,
appropriate, and effective manner.

As I feel liberated, I learn from this experience, let go of
my feelings of resentment, and move onward.

Since we have no control over other people's thoughts, feelings, or behaviors, acknowledging and owning those of our own becomes the key to maintaining control and managing our emotional state.

Taking control of our inner thoughts and self-talks empowers us to manage our emotions, control our behaviors, and reach a state of equanimity.

Just like working out strengthens our muscles; helps us build endurance; and, enables us to do things that we weren't able to do before, working through the process of genuine accountability strengths the executive part of our brain (i.e., neuroplasticity); helps us build emotional stamina; and, enables us to deal with challenging interactions the way we weren't able to do before.

*"Sow a thought, and you reap an act;
Sow an act, and you reap a habit;
Sow a habit, and you reap a character;
Sow a character, and you reap a destiny."
—Samuel Smiles*

Chapter 1

Self-Reflection:

2
What Is Happening? What Do I Feel?

When I experience stress in a relationship or in an interaction with someone, I stay nurturing and supportive towards myself and ask:

What is happening? What do I feel?

» Do I feel offended? ☐ Yes   ☐ No

If yes, proceed to Chapter 3 to examine your experience, see choices, and find a sense of resolve.

» Do I feel annoyed? ☐ Yes   ☐ No

If yes, proceed to Chapter 4 to examine your experience, see choices, and find a sense of resolve.

» Do I feel jealous? ☐ Yes   ☐ No

If yes, proceed to Chapter 5 to examine your experience, see choices, and find a sense of resolve.

» Do I feel that I have been wronged? ☐ Yes   ☐ No

If yes, proceed to Chapter 6 to examine your experience, see choices, and find a sense of resolve.

What is happening? What do I feel?

I Feel Offended (Page 13)	I Feel Annoyed (Page 37)	I Feel Jealous (Page 89)	I Feel That I've Been Wronged (Page 111)

Self-Reflection:

What Is Happening? What Do I Feel?

> *All emotions that we feel are a natural part of the human experience; Therefore, all feelings are real, valid, and acceptable.*

> *Experiencing resentment is a natural part of the human experience.*
>
> *Therefore, all our feelings of resentment (i.e., anger, hurt, frustration, disappointment, bitterness, jealousy, disgust, rage, or hatred) are real, valid, and acceptable.*
>
> *Such feelings become unhealthy and harmful only when they are left unresolved: When we hold onto them or act upon them and become reactive.*

Chapter 2

> *Acknowledge your feelings of resentment without being self-judgmental or self-critical. This way you allow your emotions to awaken you, not control you.*

> *It is when we are aware that we become empowered to discover the root cause of our emotional experience and retake our personal power and control over our lives.*

3
I Feel Offended

When I feel offended and experience the feelings of resentment (e.g., feel hurt or angry) towards someone, I stay understanding and empathetic towards myself and ask:

1. Do I believe that this person has intended to hurt my feelings? ☐ Yes ☐ No

    Do I think that this individual has taken their stress out on me? ☐ Yes ☐ No

    In other words, do I believe that this person has violated my basic human rights?
    ☐ Yes ☐ No

    If you have answered Yes to the above question, refer to Chapter 6 for further examination of your experience, seeing choices, and finding a sense of resolve.

> *Some examples of situations in which we may feel offended by other people are when they:*
> - *Give us negative feedback;*
> - *Call us on something that we said or did;*
> - *Correct us;*
> - *Offer unsolicited suggestion or advice;*
> - *Disagree with us or challenge us by asking questions;*
> - *Ignore our suggestion or advice; or,*
> - *Don't pay us the attention that we expect to receive.*

Chapter 3

2. If this person has not invaded my basic human rights, then why do I feel the way I do?

_____
_____
_____
_____
_____
_____
_____
_____
_____
_____
_____
_____
_____
_____
_____
_____
_____
_____
_____
_____
_____
_____
_____
_____
_____
_____
_____
_____

3. In view of my response to the previous question:

    Do I find myself being offended by this individual's opinion, view, observation, or belief?
    ☐ Yes ☐ No

    Do I find myself being offended by the way they *feel*?
    ☐ Yes ☐ No

    Or, do I find myself being offended by their action or inaction?
    ☐ Yes ☐ No

4. If I have answered Yes to any of the above questions, then, is it possible that I am offended by this person's way of thinking, feeling, or behaving because, deep down, it makes me feel unworthy, unimportant, inadequate, or belittled?
    ☐ Yes ☐ No

5. If yes, then why? Why does this individual's opinion, observation, belief, remark, feeling, action, or inaction make me feel that way? Could it be because it triggers *a perception of threat* to my sense of value or worth as a person and generates such inner thoughts as: *I'm being attacked, judged, and rejected*?
    ☐ Yes ☐ No

6. If yes, then could such inner thoughts and self-talks represent a false account of reality? In other words, could this be a misunderstanding? ☐ Yes ☐ No

7. If yes, then, in general, how do I tend to evaluate my self-worth and self-value:

Do I rely on others for validation or affirmation? In other words, do I need other people's approval or acknowledgment to think that I'm good enough or that I matter?
☐ Yes ☐ No

Do I have a tendency to be too hard on myself? For example, do I hold such views as: *Mistakes are bad . . . I need to be perfect to be good enough?*
☐ Yes ☐ No

If yes to any of the above questions, then why? Why do I evaluate my worth or value as a person in such a way? Why do I harbor such a mindset?

(For a more in-depth exploration of this subject matter refer to <u>Building a Strong Sense of Self: Embarking on the Journey of Change</u>.)

_____
_____
_____
_____
_____
_____
_____
_____
_____
_____

I Feel Offended

Chapter 3

> *It may be a human phenomenon that we care about what other people think of us.*
>
> *To what extent, though, do we allow 'what others think of us' to define us?*
>
> *Source: <u>The Inner Control Is the True Control Workbook, 2nd Edition</u>*

*When we are too hard on ourselves,
we may feel overwhelmed and even mentally shut
down, when someone gives us negative feedback or
calls us out on our mistakes.*

*If we have remained unaware and live on autopilot,
then we may automatically become reactive.*

*For example, we may silence the person by using
such defensive behaviors as bursting into anger,
blaming, or withdrawing.*

Chapter 3

> *When we embark on our journey of personal growth and develop a healthy sense of our self-value, we realize that we don't have to be perfect to be good enough.*
>
> *In that state of mind, when someone gives us negative feedback or calls us out on our mistakes, we become self-reflective and self-aware; overcome negative emotions; face issues; and, take appropriate actions to better ourselves.*

As humans, no one can ever be perfect,

Chapter 3

> *When we don't have a positive self-image,*
> *we constantly worry about what other people think of us.*
>
> *When we remain unaware and live on autopilot, our*
> *fears of others' judgment, rejection, and abandonment,*
> *inadvertently, drive our defensive behaviors and result*
> *in people judging, rejecting, and abandoning us.*
>
> *The problem gets even worse when we*
> *judge, reject, and abandon those who attempt to*
> *share constructive feedback with us.*
>
> *This is how we get stuck in a downward*
> *spiral of anxiety and depression.*
>
> *Believe in yourself;*
> *Build a strong sense of your Self.*

> *To overcome anger, first let go*
> *of your feelings of resentment*
> *towards yourself.*

> *Love your 'Self'*
> *unconditionally.*

> *When we remain unaware and do things without considering the consequences, then we may often encounter others' judgment, rejection, and abandonment.*
>
> *It is understandable then, that in such a state of low self-awareness, we constantly worry about what other people are thinking of us.*
>
> *Instead of allowing other people's judgment, rejection, or abandonment to define our self-image and control our lives, we retain our personal power and become self-aware by asking ourselves such questions as:*
>
> *"What is it that I am doing (or not doing) that triggers others to judge me?"*
>
> *"Since I have no control over other people, is there anything that I could change or improve in myself that would empower me to have more rewarding experiences?"*
>
> *"What are my choices?"*
>
> <u>*Accountability and Empowerment:*</u>
> <u>*A Four-Step Strategy for Overcoming Resentment*</u>

> *Believe in yourself;*
> *Retake your personal power.*

> *You are not trapped;*
> *You have choices.*

Chapter 3

> *Our goals of reaching our full potential, forming a 'lasting' and rewarding intimate relationship, and living a fulfilled life are achievable when we make great efforts to build emotional resilience.*

8. Now that I have gained more insight into myself and better understand why I feel offended, how could I let go of my feelings of resentment and reach inner peace? What are my choices?

Chapter 3

> *Hope inspires 'resolution,'*
> *Drives 'exertion,'*
> *Builds 'resilience,' and,*
> *Brings 'success.'*
>
> *When I earnestly hope to achieve a goal then I will become determined to succeed.*
>
> *This firm resolution will drive constructive behaviors: I will make 'concrete plans' and exert myself to stay committed to them.*
>
> *When I stick to my plans and reap the rewards of it, I will start believing in myself and become inspired to stay strong and persevere in the face of setbacks.*
>
> *This is how my hopes and aspirations empower me to fulfill my vision and reach my full potential.*
>
> Source: <u>The Inner Control Is the True Control Workbook, 2nd Edition</u>

> *Reach your full potential and live a fulfilled life—because you deserve nothing less.*

> *Be nurturing towards the child within;*
> *Don't be too hard on your 'Self.'*
>
> *Accept your humanness and*
> *love your 'Self' unconditionally.*
>
> *Have realistic and fair expectations of yourself.*
>
> *Keep in mind that you can never be perfect;*
> *In fact, you never have to be perfect*
> *to be adequate.*

> *Live your life by aiming for progression,*
> *not perfection.*
>
> *Believe in your 'Self.'*

Self-Reflection:

Empowering Self-Talks

> *Please pause a moment. Take a slow and deep breath. While reading the following script aloud, let each sentence deep into your conscious awareness. Then, allow the Nurturing Adult within you to guide you.*

Now that I have gained more insight into myself, I make an honest appraisal of my ways of thinking, feeling, and behaving and see my part in my unpleasant emotional experiences without being self-critical or self-deprecating.

Now,

I commit to changing my ways of thinking:
I change those inner thoughts and self-talks that
generate my feelings of resentment and
drive my defensive behaviors.

I do so through cultivating such virtues
as compassion and logical reasoning that support
self-love and foster emotional resilience.

I allow these sound principles to govern
my ways of thinking and serve as a foundation
upon which I define, measure, and evaluate
my self-value and self-worth.

Such a constructive mindset empowers me to separate
my character flaws from the person within me.

Now, I see my True Self.

Chapter 3

Now,

I can affirm and acknowledge my Self.

Now, I can see that:

√ My mistakes don't define me: *Mistakes are opportunities for growth and transformation.*

√ My character flaws don't define me: *I learned my faulty ways of thinking, feeling, and behaving in the early years of my childhood; therefore, I can change them.*

√ My imperfections or limitations (humanness) don't define me: *As humans, no one is perfect.*

√ I am adequate: *I am inherently worthy.*

Now,

I no longer judge or label my *Self* as inadequate, unworthy, bad, or inferior . . .

Now, I love my Self unconditionally.

As I build a strong sense of my *Self* and develop emotional resilience, I come to experience rewarding relationships.

Now, I find my inner strength and feel a sense of inner calmness.

> Please stay in the present moment!

> *Please pause a moment. Take a slow and deep breath. While reading the following script aloud, let each sentence deep into your conscious awareness. Then, allow the Nurturing Adult within you to guide you.*

Now that I have gained more knowledge on my path to personal growth, I see that, as a mature adult, it is *my responsibility* to affirm and acknowledge my *Self*.

Now,

I don't need to be validated by others to know that I'm good enough or that I matter.

I don't need to receive attention to know that I'm important.

I don't need to be right or win arguments to know that I'm adequate.

I don't need other people to like, approve, admire, or praise me to know that I am worthy.

I don't need other people to notice or acknowledge me to know that I matter.

Now that I am able to affirm, acknowledge, and love my *Self* unconditionally, my internal thoughts and dialogues are no longer like this:

> *I should think, feel, or behave in a certain way so that everyone likes me, approves of me, or regards me as adequate or worthy.*

Chapter 3

Now,

I can separate my character flaws from my *Self* (*The Person Within*) and understand that people's rejection of my behavior is not a rejection of *Me*.

Now,

I can hear and consider other people's feedback, constructive criticism, advice, or suggestions with an open mind and a grateful heart.

Now,

I can stay non-reactive when I'm held accountable for the consequences of my mistakes.

Now,

I feel a sense of inner strength and calmness.

Please stay in the present moment!

> *Please pause a moment. Take a slow and deep breath. While reading the following script aloud, let each sentence deep into your conscious awareness. Then, allow the Nurturing Adult within you to guide you.*

In sum,

When I feel offended by someone's way of thinking, feeling, or behaving, I refocus and look inwardly.

Refocusing and holding myself accountable for my ways of thinking, feeling, and behaving liberates me and empowers me to retain my personal power and see choices.

Now,

I work towards building a stronger sense of my *Self*.

Now,

I let go of my feelings of resentment and commit to my new learnings.

Now,

I am empowered to reach a state of equanimity.

> *Please stay in the present moment!*

My Self-Talks

This section is offered for you to craft your own self-talk scripts. It is highly recommended that you design these dialogues in a manner in which you could revisit them during future stressful times—when you feel offended and experience a sense of loss of control. Recalling the tools that helped you in the past will enable you to let go of your feelings of resentment and control its downward spiral in a shorter span of time.

My Self-Talks

Chapter 3

4
I Feel Annoyed

When I feel annoyed and experience the feelings of resentment (e.g., feel irritated, frustrated, or angry) towards someone, I stay understanding and empathetic towards myself and ask:

1. Do I believe that this person is intentionally trying to annoy me?
   ☐ Yes ☐ No

   Do I believe that this person is violating my basic human rights in any other way?
   ☐ Yes ☐ No

   If you have answered Yes to the above questions, refer to Chapter 6 for further examination of your experience, seeing choices, and finding a sense of resolve.

> *Some examples of situations in which we may feel annoyed with other people are when they:*
> » *Seek attention, affirmation, or acknowledgment;*
> » *Display emotions openly;*
> » *Become overly attentive to us;*
> » *Ask questions;*
> » *Make mistakes;*
> » *Appear self-confident;*
> » *Speak assertively;*
> » *Disagree with our views or opinions; or,*
> » *Hold beliefs that we strongly disagree with.*

2. If this person is not violating my basic human rights, then why do I feel the way I do?

All of the emotions that one feels are a natural part of the human experience; Therefore, our feelings of annoyance are real, valid, and acceptable.

A 'non-judgmental and non-critical' acknowledgment of our feelings helps direct our attention to the root cause of our emotional experience: our mindset.

When we refocus and become aware of our internal thoughts and dialogues that generate our feelings of annoyance, we become empowered to see choices.

3. In view of my response to the previous question, what exactly is it about this person that annoys me?

   Is it their way of thinking, feeling, or behaving? In other words:

   Do I find myself being annoyed by this individual's opinion, view, observation, or belief?
   ☐ Yes   ☐ No

   Do I find myself being annoyed with the way they *feel*?
   ☐ Yes   ☐ No

   Or, do I find myself being annoyed with their action or inaction?
   ☐ Yes   ☐ No

   If I have answered Yes to any of the above questions, then, do I basically feel annoyed because this person thinks, feels, or behaves in a certain manner?
   ☐ Yes   ☐ No

4. If yes, then why?

   Why does this individual's opinion, view, belief, remark, feeling, action, or inaction make me feel the way I do?

   If I search deep within, would I find myself experiencing one or more of the following situations?

   Please see Scenarios 1 through 9 that are presented on the next several pages.

Scenario 1

I feel irritated because I perceive this person as being excessively attentive and overly focused on my concerns and problems.

In other words, I find this individual's way of thinking, feeling, or behaving annoying because it makes me feel controlled.

In this situation, I unconsciously *redirect* my feelings of anxiety—that are triggered by my deep-seated fears of losing control and being trapped (fear of engulfment)—and become resentful of the person.

🍂 🍂 🍂

If this is the case, then, when I look deeper within, do I find myself *relying on* other people for support, reassurance, and advice in times of stress?
☐ Yes   ☐ No

If yes, then do I generally tend to follow the suggestions that I'm offered without considering the advice of my own? ☐ Yes   ☐ No

If yes, then why? Why do I relinquish my personal power and control and encourage others to assume responsibility for me when I'm stressed?

(For a more in-depth exploration of this subject matter refer to <u>Building a Strong Sense of Self: Embarking on the Journey of Change</u>.)

Chapter 4

> *When faced with setbacks or difficult times, believe in your Self.*
>
> *Retain your personal power and trust your inner strength.*

> *You are not trapped;*
> *You have choices.*
>
> *You are in control of your own lives: You have control over your ways of thinking (inner control) that drive the choices that you make.*

> *During setbacks:*
>
> *OBSERVE,*
> *NURTURE, and*
> *EMPOWER your Self!*
>
> *Observe your Self and acknowledge your feelings in a non-judgmental manner;*
>
> *Nurture your Self by being supportive and empathetic towards yourself; and,*
>
> *Empower your Self by engaging in inspirational and motivational self-talks (i.e., "I can do this!").*

Chapter 4

Now that I have gained more insight into myself, how can I overcome my feelings of annoyance and gain inner peace? What are my choices?

Scenario 2

I find this person's way of thinking, feeling, or behaving annoying because it deviates from my social norms (i.e., the standards and values that are held by the people that I associate with, such as my friends).

In other words, I feel annoyed because this person doesn't think, feel, or behave in a manner in which people in my social circle deem appropriate or proper.

In this situation, I unconsciously *redirect* my feelings of anxiety— that are triggered by my subconscious fear of other people's judgment, rejection, and abandonment— and become annoyed with the individual.

※ ※ ※

If this is the case, then do I generally need to fit in or be accepted by others, in particular, by people whom I relate to or perceive as worthy, to feel a sense of inner normalcy?
☐ Yes   ☐ No

If yes, then why? Why do I harbor such a mindset?
(For a more in-depth exploration of this subject matter refer to Building a Strong Sense of Self: Embarking on the Journey of Change.)

_____
_____
_____
_____

Chapter 4

> *When we need others to affirm us (that we are good enough) or acknowledge us (that we matter), then we may have to work hard to please everyone…*
>
> *Retain your personal power:*
> *Believe in yourself; Affirm and acknowledge yourself.*
>
> *Source: <u>The Inner Control Is the True Control Workbook, 2nd Edition</u>*

> *Let us define our 'Self' by a set of constructive and sound standards and values that fit our 'True Self.'*
>
> *Let us not allow other people's standards or values to define, control, or limit us.*

Chapter 4

Now that I have gained more insight into myself and better understand why I feel the way I do, then how can I overcome my feelings of annoyance and gain inner peace? What are my choices?

Scenario 3

I find this person's way of thinking, feeling, or behaving annoying since it doesn't meet my expectations, wishes, or desires.

In other words, I feel irritated because I don't think that I matter or that I'm important to this person.

In this situation, I unconsciously *redirect* my feelings of anxiety— that are triggered by my subconscious fear of being unworthy or unimportant—and become resentful of the individual.

☙ ☙ ☙

If this is the case, then do I generally rely on others for validation or affirmation?
☐ Yes   ☐ No

Do I need other people to attend to my feelings, needs, or desires to think that I matter or that I am important?
☐ Yes   ☐ No

Do I need others to agree with me, follow my advice, or conform to my beliefs to gain a sense of inner normalcy?
☐ Yes   ☐ No

If I have answered Yes to any of the above questions, then why? Why do I harbor such a mindset?

(For a more in-depth exploration of this subject matter, refer to <u>Building a Strong Sense of Self: Embarking on the Journey of Change</u>.)

Chapter 4

> *As a mature adult, I am responsible for my own emotional health and well-being... It is my responsibility to acknowledge and affirm myself... I am responsible for my happiness...*
>
> Source: <u>Building a Strong Sense of Self: Embarking on the Journey of Change</u>

> *When I focus on my own self, I am not being self-absorbed.*
>
> *When I make a healthy environment for myself, I am not being antisocial.*
>
> *When I engage in self-care, I am not being selfish.*
>
> *When I stop sacrificing my physical, mental, or emotional needs to attend to those of others, I am not being egocentric.*
>
> *So, without being enabling, I will be kind and understanding to the child in me; It is only then that I can be the best I could ever be.*
>
> *When I am the best that I could ever be, then I can be patient, tolerant, and understanding.*
>
> *When I am the best that I could ever be, then I can genuinely care for other people.*
>
> *When I am the best that I could ever be, then I can give without expecting anything in return.*
>
> *When I am the best that I could ever be, then I can see that others matter, too.*
>
> *So, I Matter!*
>
> Source: <u>Building a Strong Sense of Self: Embarking on the Journey of Change</u>

Chapter 4

Now that I have gained more insight into myself and better understand why I feel the way I do, then how can I overcome my feelings of annoyance and gain inner peace? What are my choices?

Scenario 4

I find the person's way of thinking, feeling, or behaving annoying because it deviates from my standards.

In other words, I feel frustrated since this individual's performance doesn't meet my standards of perfection or flawlessness.

This incident triggers memories (associated with past aversive events) and evokes such deep-seated fears as fear of failure, making mistakes, being imperfect, or being judged, rejected, and abandoned by others.

In this situation, I unconsciously *redirect* my feelings of anxiety—as I fear and anticipate an unpleasant experience—and get irritated with the person.

‌🙵 🙵 🙵

If this is the case, then do I generally tend to strive for perfection to gain a sense of inner normalcy?
☐ Yes   ☐ No

If yes, then why? Why do I harbor such a mindset?
(For a more in-depth exploration of this subject matter, refer to <u>Building a Strong Sense of Self: Embarking on the Journey of Change</u>.)

_____
_____
_____
_____

Chapter 4

Nothing may help us feel more grounded than facing our own humanness.

Nothing may help us forgive more readily than accepting other people's humanness.

Source: <u>The Inner Control Is the True Control Workbook, 2nd Edition</u>

Let us accept our humanness and love ourselves unconditionally.

Let us establish and set fair and reasonable expectations for ourselves that are based on excellence, and not perfection.

Accepting that we don't have to be perfect to be good enough will liberate us.

Now, let us extend this new outlook to people around us and have realistic expectations for them.

Chapter 4

Now that I have gained more insight into myself and better understand why I feel the way I do, then how can I overcome my feelings of annoyance and gain inner peace? What are my choices?

Scenario 5

Although it is not violating my rights or the rights of people who need my defending, I find this person's way of thinking, feeling, or behaving annoying because it deviates from my moral or ethical values.

In other words, I feel frustrated because this individual doesn't think, feel, or behave in a way that I deem right or acceptable.

In this situation, I unconsciously *redirect* my own feelings of anxiety— that are triggered by my subconscious fear of punishment—and become annoyed with the person.

If this is the case, then do I generally tend to hold myself and others accountable to a set of binary-based rules of right and wrong? ☐ Yes ☐ No

Do I need to maintain control and bring peace, order, and justice in my environment to gain a sense of inner normalcy? ☐ Yes ☐ No

Do I need to be all good to feel worthy and deserving of receiving love? ☐ Yes ☐ No

If I have answered Yes to any of the above questions, then why? Why do I harbor such a mindset?

(For a more in-depth exploration of this subject matter, refer to <u>Building a Strong Sense of Self: Embarking on the Journey of Change</u>.)

Chapter 4

> *We are inherently worthy.*
>
> *We don't have to be all good to be deserving of love.*
>
> *We are all worthy of love and respect.*
>
> *Let us love ourselves unconditionally.*

Chapter 4

> *We can effect change far more effectively when we express ourselves in a non-reactive, empathetic, and respectful manner.*

> *"When you find no solution to a problem, it's probably not a problem to be solved, but rather a truth to be accepted."*
> —Gyalwa Rinpoche

*Tolerance doesn't mean appeasing others;
Nor does it mean stopping ourselves from
expressing our views or asserting our rights.*

*Tolerance is about letting go of our feelings of
annoyance so that we could contain the
urge to fix or control other people.*

"What is stress? It's the gap between
our expectations and reality. More the gap,
the more the stress. So expect nothing
and accept everything."
—Anonymous

Chapter 4

Now that I have gained more insight into myself and better understand why I feel the way I do, then how can I overcome my feelings of annoyance and gain inner peace? What are my choices?

Scenario 6

I find this person's way of thinking, feeling, or behaving annoying because it makes me become self-conscious.

In other words, I feel irritated because I think that this person is judging me.

In this situation, I unconsciously *redirect* my feelings of anxiety— that are triggered by my deep-seated fears of inadequacy and others' rejection and abandonment— and become resentful of the person.

❦ ❦ ❦

If this is the case, then do I generally define or evaluate my value or worth as a person based on what others think of me?
☐ Yes   ☐ No

Do I need other people to think highly of me to feel that I'm adequate?
☐ Yes   ☐ No

If I have answered Yes to any of the above questions, then why? Why do I harbor such a mindset?

(For a more in-depth exploration of this subject matter, refer to <u>Building a Strong Sense of Self: Embarking on the Journey of Change</u>.)

_____
_____
_____

Chapter 4

> *Let us make a distinction between*
> *'worrying about what others are thinking of us' and*
> *'being concerned about how our behaviors are impacting them.'*

> *What other people think of me is not for me to own.*
>
> *Source: <u>Accountability and Empowerment:</u>*
> *<u>A Four-Step Strategy for Overcoming Resentment</u>*

> *"In order to change the nature of things, either within yourself or in others, one should change, not the events, but those thoughts which created those events." —Leo Tolstoy*

Chapter 4

Now that I have gained more insight into myself and better understand why I feel the way I do, then how can I overcome my feelings of annoyance and gain inner peace? What are my choices?

Scenario 7

I am annoyed because this person appears to be overly confident, assertive, and condescending.

In other words, when I search deep within, I find this person's way of thinking, feeling, or behaving irritating because it makes me feel insignificant.

In this situation, I unconsciously redirect my feelings of anxiety— that are triggered by such subconscious fears as fear of being less than others or fear of loss of status— and become resentful of the person.

☙ ☙ ☙

If this is the case, then, in general, do I need to be better than others to feel a sense of inner normalcy?
☐ Yes   ☐ No

Do I need to be all knowing to think that I'm good enough?
☐ Yes   ☐ No

If I have answered Yes to any of the above questions, then why? Why do I harbor such a mindset?

(For a more in-depth exploration of this subject matter, refer to <u>Building a Strong Sense of Self: Embarking on the Journey of Change</u>.)

_____
_____
_____
_____

Chapter 4

*When we overcome the feelings of 'shame,'
then we become free to feel the emotion of 'guilt.'*

*When we allow ourselves to feel the painful emotion of guilt,
then we become enabled to discover our character flaws.*

*When we work on our flaws and better ourselves,
then we experience rewarding outcomes.*

*When we accumulate positive experiences,
then we gain the ability to form a healthy self-image.*

*When we build a strong sense of our 'self,'
then we allow ourselves to feel all emotions: shame, guilt . . .
This is because, in that state of high self-esteem,
we are controlled by the compassion in our heart
and the logical brain in our mind.*

*When we are emotionally resilient and able to manage
the emotions of shame and guilt,
then we don't blame other people for our own
thoughts, feelings, actions, or inactions.
Rather, we forgive ourselves for our mistakes,
take responsibility for our choices, and
commit to new ways of being.*

*At that phase in our lives,
where we are humbled by our humanness,
we don't have the need to be perfect, better, all knowing,
or all good to gain a sense of inner normalcy.*

*For a more in-depth exploration of this subject matter,
please refer to <u>Building a Strong Sense of Self</u>:
<u>Embarking on the Journey of Change.</u>*

---

*Let the emotion of shame awaken you,
not enslave or control you.*

Chapter 4

Now that I have gained more insight into myself and better understand why I feel the way I do, then how can I overcome my feelings of annoyance and gain inner peace? What are my choices?

Scenario 8

I find this person's way of thinking, feeling, or behaving annoying because it disrupts my ritual norms.

In other words, I feel frustrated because this individual disturbs my [daily] routines that help me gain a sense of control, security, and inner normalcy.

In this situation, I unconsciously redirect my feelings of anxiety— that are triggered by my subconscious fears of lack of certainty, predictability, and control—and become resentful of the person.

🙰 🙰 🙰

If this is the case, then, in general, do I need to strictly adhere to a set of rituals or have plans, order, and structure in my life to gain a sense of security and inner normalcy?
☐ Yes   ☐ No

If yes, then why do I have such a need?

(For a more in-depth exploration of this subject matter, refer to <u>Building a Strong Sense of Self: Embarking on the Journey of Change</u>.)

_____
_____
_____
_____
_____
_____

Chapter 4

> *We control our environment when we are unable to control the deep-seated emotion of fear:*
>
> *Anticipating undesirable experiences
> (such as loss, failure, or others' judgment, rejection, abandonment, or angry reactions)
> evokes the emotion of fear,
> generates the feelings of anxiety, and
> drives an urge to control our environment (e.g., people).*

> *The inner control is the true control:*
>
> *Gaining control over our thoughts and self-talks will empower us to see choices (e.g., set and maintain healthy personal boundaries) and gain control over our lives.*

Chapter 4

Now that I have gained more insight into myself and better understand why I feel the way I do, then how can I overcome my feelings of annoyance and gain inner peace? What are my choices?

Scenario 9

I find this individual's way of thinking, feeling, or behaving annoying because it deviates from my realm of understanding: *"This person doesn't think, feel, or behave the way they should."*

In other words, I feel frustrated because this person does not think, feel, or behave like me or others whom I can relate to.

In this situation, I unconsciously redirect my feelings of anxiety— that are triggered by my subconscious fears of the unknown and lack of control—and become irritated with the person.

If this is the case, then, do I generally have a need for familiarity to feel a sense of security and inner normalcy?
☐ Yes   ☐ No

Do I usually have a difficult time adapting to change?
☐ Yes   ☐ No

If I have answered Yes to any of the above questions, then why do I?

(For a more in-depth exploration of this subject matter, refer to <u>Building a Strong Sense of Self: Embarking on the Journey of Change</u>.)

_____
_____
_____

Chapter 4

*To adjust to changes in our environment, we connect
with our heart, not our mind;
For the compassion in our heart brings us inner peace,
while the thoughts in our mind evoke fear of the unknown
and generate feelings of anxiety and resentment.*

*Let us take back our control;
Let us not allow our fears to control us.*

*When we get to know other people,
we better understand why they think, feel, and act
the way they do.*

*Gaining insight into others liberates us
from our fears.*

Chapter 4

Now that I have gained more insight into myself and better understand why I feel the way I do, then how can I overcome my feelings of annoyance and gain inner peace? What are my choices?

I Feel Annoyed

Other Possible Scenario

Chapter 4

Now that I have gained more insight into myself and better understand why I feel the way I do, then how can I overcome my feelings of annoyance and gain inner peace? What are my choices?

> Anxiety may be a 'learned' behavior.

As children, we naturally experience anxiety and instinctively express our unpleasant feelings outwardly when we are faced with stressful or undesirable situations.

When the display of anxiety becomes reinforced by our immediate environment (either through passivity or modeling by a caretaker), then we don't learn healthy ways of managing our emotions during times of stress.

In such a case as this, we 'learn' to continue to exhibit anxiety in order to control the stressors that trigger our inner unrest.

That is to say, we learn to display anxiety (i.e., get irritable, restless, or angry) as a way to avoid facing events that we find overwhelming or unpleasant. In essence, by exhibiting anxiety, we are saying, "I feel helpless."

When remained unchecked, this defensive behavior becomes conditioned in us as we transition into adulthood.

As adults, when the associative part of our brain becomes triggered by an event (i.e., a similar situation that we found overwhelming or undesirable as a child), our emotional brain generates an emotional response:

The stimulus (i.e., the event) evokes the emotion of fear, generates feelings of anxiety, and drives anxious behaviors.

In other words, when we remain unaware, we may not realize that the Child in us exhibits anxiety during times of stress in order to control the environment and gain a sense of inner normalcy.

> Anxiety serves a purpose: It helps us control our environment and gain a sense of security 'at a given moment in time.'

> When we experience anxiety, we become aware of our feelings and internal thoughts. Then, we allow the thinking part of our brain (the Nurturing Parent within) to help us reach a state of inner calmness. This is when we will find answers and see choices.

Self-Reflection:

Empowering Self-Talks

> *Please pause a moment. Take a slow and deep breath. While reading the following script aloud, let each sentence deep into your conscious awareness. Then, allow the Nurturing Adult within you to guide you.*

Now that I have gained more insight into myself, I make an honest appraisal of my ways of thinking, feeling, and behaving and see my part in my unpleasant emotional experiences without being self-critical or self-deprecating.

Now,

I commit to changing my ways of thinking:

I change those inner thoughts and self-talks that generate my feelings of annoyance and drive my defensive behaviors.

To carry out this task,
I cultivate such virtues as flexibility, adaptability, patience, and fairness that help me regulate my emotions, stay separate, and maintain healthy personal boundaries with others.

I allow these sound principles to govern my ways of thinking and serve as a foundation upon which I perceive and respond to other people's ways of thinking, feeling, or behaving (their character traits).

Chapter 4

Now,

When I experience the feelings of anxiety,
the compassion that comes from *the Nurturing Parent Within* guides me on the path to a state of inner peace.

Now,

When I experience the feelings of annoyance, the wisdom that comes from *the Adult Within* helps me see that some of my rules are not enforceable:
I cannot change people or expect that they think, feel, or behave in a certain manner.

Now, my inner thoughts and self-talks
are like this:

*As long as my basic human rights
(or those of others who need my defending)
are not violated, people have a right to their own
ways of thinking, feeling, and behaving.*

Now,

I feel a sense of control and inner calmness.

> *Please stay in the present moment!*

> *Please pause a moment. Take a slow and deep breath. While reading the following script aloud, let each sentence deep into your conscious awareness. Then, allow the Nurturing Adult within you to guide you.*

In sum,

When I feel annoyed because someone thinks, feels, or behaves in a certain manner, I refocus and look inwardly:

I own my feelings and hold myself accountable for my ways of thinking.

This self-accountability empowers me to:

Retake my personal power, become aware, and see choices;

Stay separate and maintain healthy boundaries with other people;

Form rewarding relationships; and,

Experience a state of equanimity, inner harmony, and total wellness.

> *Please stay in the present moment!*

My Self-Talks

This section is offered for you to craft your own self-talk scripts. It is highly recommended that you design these dialogues in a manner in which you could revisit them during future stressful times—when you feel annoyed and experience a sense of loss of control. Recalling the tools that helped you in the past will enable you to let go of your feelings of resentment and control its downward spiral in a shorter span of time.

My Self-Talks

Chapter 4

5
I Feel Jealous

When I feel jealous of someone and experience the feelings of resentment (e.g., feel bitter and resentful), I stay understanding and empathetic towards myself and ask:

1. Why am I jealous of this person?

_____
_____
_____
_____
_____
_____
_____
_____
_____
_____
_____
_____
_____
_____
_____
_____
_____
_____
_____
_____

2. Do I feel envious of this person because they possess something that I don't have or perceive that I lack, such as a certain physical attribute or personality trait, wealth, accomplishment, status, popularity, or an intimate relationship?
☐ Yes   ☐ No

3. If yes, then do I experience any other feelings besides feelings of jealousy and resentment? For example, if I search deep within, would I find myself feeling:

Sad?	☐ Yes	☐ No
Unhappy?	☐ Yes	☐ No
Hopeless?	☐ Yes	☐ No
Disappointed?	☐ Yes	☐ No
Frustrated?	☐ Yes	☐ No

Any others feelings?
_____
_____
_____

4. If I experience any of the above feelings, then why do I? Why do I feel that way?

_____
_____
_____
_____
_____

I Feel Jealous

Chapter 5

> *All of the emotions that we feel are a natural part of our human experience.*
>
> *Therefore, all of our feelings are real, valid, and acceptable.*
>
> *Our feelings of envy or jealousy become unhealthy only when they are left unresolved: when we bottle up or when we act upon them and become reactive.*
>
> *This non-judgmental perspective helps us focus on the root cause of our emotional experience (i.e., our ways of thinking) without being self-critical or self-deprecating.*

5. Could I be feeling the way I do because I'm making a comparison between myself and this individual? In other words, do I feel the way I do because I am comparing myself and perceiving this person as being superior, better, or more special than me? ☐ Yes ☐ No

6. If yes, then do I view myself as being less (e.g., less special or less worthy) than this individual only because of what they possess, such as their certain physical attribute or personal characteristic, accomplishment, success, wealth, status, popularity, or relationship? ☐ Yes ☐ No

7. If yes, then why do I hold such an image of my *Self*? Could it be because I define and evaluate my worth or value as a person based on such factors as these? ☐ Yes ☐ No

8. If yes, then could such a poor self-image (*I'm not good enough because I don't possess what this person has*) subconsciously evoke the deep-seated emotion of shame and generate feelings of anxiety (i.e., fear of loss of status or others' judgment, rejection, and abandonment)? ☐ Yes ☐ No

9. If yes, then is it possible that, at the subconscious level, the feelings of anxiety trigger my conditioned defense mechanism and therefore, I redirect my feelings of inadequacy or inferiority towards the person and become resentful of them? ☐ Yes ☐ No

10. If yes, then, in general, do I have a tendency to evaluate (i.e., constantly compare myself with others) and judge myself harshly?   ☐ Yes   ☐ No

11. If yes, then why? Why do I tend to be too hard on myself?

12. Could it be that I have a habit of constantly comparing myself to other people because I harbor such internal thoughts and self-talks as: *I need to be better, superior, or more special than others to be good enough*?
☐ Yes ☐ No

13. If yes, then why? Why do I evaluate my worth or value as a person in such a way? Why do I harbor such a mindset?

    (For a more in-depth exploration of this subject matter refer to <u>Building a Strong Sense of Self: Embarking on the Journey of Change</u>.)

Chapter 5

I Feel Jealous

> *When we define our self-image based on the concept of exceptionalism—we need to be better, superior, or more special than others to be good enough—then we have to constantly compare ourselves with other people to make sure that we 'are' better, superior, or more special than them.*

Chapter 5

> *There is no path to total wellness when we always have to worry: "Am I special? What do others think of me? Am I their favorite? Do people in my social circle rely on me? Do they enjoy my company more than they do others'?"*

14. Now that I have gained more insight into myself and better understand why I feel the way I do, then how can I overcome my feelings of jealousy, reach inner peace, and achieve my optimal potential? What are my choices?

_____
_____
_____
_____
_____
_____
_____
_____
_____
_____
_____
_____
_____
_____
_____
_____
_____
_____
_____
_____
_____
_____
_____
_____
_____

Chapter 5

> *How do we deal with the natural human emotion of jealousy?*
>
> *Do we allow our feelings of envy or jealousy to control our lives?*
>
> *Or,*
>
> *Do we retake our control and choose to be inspired by people whom we feel envious of?*
>
> *We always have a choice.*

> *While I cherish my strengths and take pride in my accomplishments, I realize that my advantages, greatness, gifts, talents, or skills do not define me or make me superior.*
>
> *While I support myself in turning my weaknesses into my strengths, I realize that my imperfections, flaws, or limitations do not define me or make me inferior.*
>
> Source: <u>Building a Strong Sense of Self: Embarking on the Journey of Change</u>

Chapter 5

Self-Reflection:

Empowering Self-Talks

> *Please pause a moment. Take a slow and deep breath. While reading the following script aloud, let each sentence deep into your conscious awareness. Then, allow the Nurturing Adult within you to guide you.*

Now that I have gained more insight into myself, I make an honest appraisal of my ways of thinking, feeling, and behaving and see my part in my unpleasant emotional experiences without being self-critical or self-deprecating.

Now,

I commit to changing the internal thoughts and self-talks that generate my feelings of jealousy and drive my conditioned defense mechanism.

I work towards achieving this goal by cultivating such virtues as logical reasoning and compassion that support self-empathy.

I allow such sound principles
to serve as a foundation upon which I define
my value and worth as a person.

Now,

I no longer define or evaluate my *self*
based on such factors as my physical attributes,
accomplishments, wealth, race,
popularity, or social status.

Chapter 5

Now,

I allow *the Nurturing Parent* within me to govern my internal thoughts and self-talks.

The self-compassion that comes from *the Nurturing Parent Within* empowers me to see that:
I am inherently worthy.

Now,

I see a true image of my *Self*.

The insight into my *True Self* gives me the clarity to see the truth:

I don't have to be better or superior to anyone to be good enough.

I am neither inferior nor superior to anyone; I am equal to others.

I am adequate.

Now,

I can affirm and acknowledge my *Self* and love myself unconditionally.

Now,

The self-compassion that comes from *the Nurturing Parent Within* stops me from constantly comparing myself with others.

Now that I experience rewarding relationships, I am empowered to focus on myself and reach my full potential.

Now,

I feel a sense of inner calmness.

> *Please stay in the present moment!*

> *Please pause a moment. Take a slow and deep breath. While reading the following script aloud, let each sentence deep into your conscious awareness. Then, allow the Nurturing Adult within you to guide you.*

In sum:

When I compare myself with someone and experience feelings of jealousy, I refocus and work on building a stronger sense of my *self*.

Now,

I realize that when I affirm myself and remember that *I'm inherently worthy,* I will not have a need to compare myself with others.

Now,

I feel liberated, inspired, and empowered to fulfill my hopes and aspirations.

Now,

I experience a state of equanimity and inner harmony.

This state of 'being' leads to rewarding outcomes and a sense of well-being.

> *Please stay in the present moment!*

My Self-Talks

This section is offered for you to craft your own self-talk scripts. It is highly recommended that you design these dialogues in a manner in which you could revisit them during future stressful times—when you feel jealous and experience a sense of loss of control. Recalling the tools that helped you in the past will enable you to let go of your feelings of resentment and control its downward spiral in a shorter span of time.

_____
_____
_____
_____
_____
_____
_____
_____
_____
_____
_____
_____
_____
_____
_____
_____
_____
_____
_____
_____
_____
_____
_____
_____
_____

Chapter 5

My Self-Talks

Chapter 5

For a more in-depth exploration of the root causes of the feelings of jealousy as well as seeing more choices in overcoming them, please refer to:

<u>Accountability and Empowerment:</u>
<u>A Four-Step Strategy for Overcoming Resentment</u>.

6
I Feel That I Have Been Wronged

When I discover that I am angry and resentful towards someone because I believe that I have been wronged by them, I remain secure, strong, and non-reactive and ask:

1. Why do I feel that I've been wronged? Do I believe that this person has unwittingly or intentionally violated my basic human rights? ☐ Yes ☐ No

> *Some examples of situations in which we are wronged by others are when they, consciously or unconsciously, violate our basic human rights. These fundamental rights may be our:*
>
> » *Verbal rights (our freedom of speech): We have the right to ask questions and freely express our thoughts, feelings, opinions, hopes, and desires.*
>
> » *Physical rights: We have the right to our body; physical space (e.g., physical privacy); personal space (e.g., the food that we put in our mouth); and, choice of attire, make-up, and expression of our gender identity.*
>
> » *Emotional rights: We have the right to be treated with respect, dignity, equality, and equity. In other words, we rightfully expect that others to treat us fairly and respectfully regardless of such factors as our physical attributes or characteristics (e.g., skin tone or color, weight, or height), background, intelligence, level of education, accomplishment, wealth, gender identity, sexual orientation, religious or spiritual beliefs, or ways of thinking or feeling about a situation.*
>
> » *Sexual rights: We have the right to make such decisions as how, when, where, and with whom to have sexual activity.*
>
> » *Spiritual rights: We have the right to choose our religious or spiritual values, beliefs, and practices.*
>
> » *Material rights: We have the right to our belongings and possessions (e.g., cell phone, computer, and clothes) and physical environment (e.g., car and place of living or working).*

Chapter 6

> *Our right to free expression may be limited by our intentions.*

> *Aren't we violating others' emotional rights when the expression of our feelings or thoughts comes from a place of resentment (e.g., when the intention is to punish or control other people's behaviors)?*

> *Aren't we practicing our basic human rights when the harsh truth that we express comes from a good place in our heart (e.g., when the intention is to repair a relationship)?*

> *The harsh truth that is expressed from a good place in our heart, rather than a judgment that comes from a resentful place in our mind, is kind, constructive, and freeing.*
>
> Source: <u>Accountability and Empowerment: A Four-Step Strategy for Overcoming Resentment</u>

2. If I have answered Yes to the previous question, then which of my rights have been overstepped?

Has this person, unwittingly or intentionally, violated my *verbal rights*? ☐ Yes ☐ No

Has this person, unwittingly or intentionally, violated my *physical rights*? ☐ Yes ☐ No

Has this person, unwittingly or intentionally, violated my *emotional rights*? ☐ Yes ☐ No

Has this person, unwittingly or intentionally, violated my *sexual rights*? ☐ Yes ☐ No

Has this person, unwittingly or intentionally, violated my *spiritual rights*? ☐ Yes ☐ No

Has this person, unwittingly or intentionally, violated my *material rights*? ☐ Yes ☐ No

---

A WORD OF CAUTION!

Please be informed that this chapter is not designed for the victims of rape or sexual assault or for those who were physically or sexually abused as children. While working through this section may help, seeking professional support and guidance is strongly recommended for reaching a true state of emotional healing in such cases.

3. If I've answered Yes to any of the previous questions, (meaning that one or more of my basic human rights have been violated by this person), then how have I protected myself and asserted my rights? Have I expressed my true feelings clearly, and directly in a non-reactive manner? Have I set appropriate limits in a healthy and effective way?
☐ Yes ☐ No

4. If *no*, then why not? Why haven't I expressed myself? Why haven't I defended my basic human rights?

_____
_____
_____
_____
_____
_____
_____
_____
_____
_____
_____
_____
_____
_____
_____
_____

5. Could it be that I've held back from asserting myself because I feel anticipatory anxiety? For example:

» Is it possible that I have not expressed my true feelings because I worry or fear that this person would become angry or retaliatory?
☐ Yes   ☐ No

If yes, then why is that? Why do I worry about this individual's reactive behavior (i.e., their conditioned defense mechanism)? Why do I give them power over me? Could it be because I see myself as a powerless or weak person?
☐ Yes   ☐ No

If yes, then why? Why do I harbor such a self-image?
(For a more in-depth exploration of this subject matter refer to <u>Accountability and Empowerment: A Four-Step Strategy for Overcoming Resentment</u>.)

_____
_____
_____
_____
_____
_____
_____
_____
_____
_____
_____
_____

» Is it possible that I have not expressed my true feelings because I worry or fear that *others around me* would judge, reject, and abandon me?
☐ Yes ☐ No

If yes, then why is that? Why do I worry about what other people think? Why do I give others power over me? Could it be because I define my self-worth based on *what others think of me*?
☐ Yes ☐ No

If yes, then why? Why do I harbor such a mindset?

(For a more in-depth exploration of this subject matter refer to <u>Building a Strong Sense of Self: Embarking on the Journey of Change</u>.)

_____
_____
_____
_____
_____
_____
_____
_____
_____
_____
_____
_____
_____
_____
_____
_____

» Is it possible that I have not expressed my true feelings because I worry or fear that I would lose this person's approval, validation, friendship, or love (i.e., fear of abandonment)?
☐ Yes ☐ No

If yes, then why is that? Why do I worry about losing this individual's approval, validation, friendship, or love? Why do I give this person power over me? Could it be because I am emotionally dependent on them (i.e., I need their acknowledgment and affirmation to feel that I'm adequate and worthy)?
☐ Yes ☐ No

If yes, then why? Why do I harbor such a mindset?
(For a more in-depth exploration of this subject matter refer to <u>Building a Strong Sense of Self: Embarking on the Journey of Change</u>.)

_____
_____
_____
_____
_____
_____
_____
_____
_____
_____
_____
_____

Chapter 6

» Are there any other reasons that would explain why I have held back from expressing my true feelings and asserting myself?

_____
_____
_____
_____
_____
_____
_____
_____
_____
_____
_____
_____
_____
_____
_____
_____
_____
_____
_____
_____
_____
_____
_____
_____

6. In general, how do I tend to guard and protect my basic human rights in my relationships with others?

7. In general, do I *freely* share my thoughts, views, and feelings with others in my relationships?
   ☐ Yes ☐ No

   If *no*, then why not?

8. Do I generally set clear and appropriate personal boundaries *'with'* others? In other words, do people in my relationships have a clear understanding of what my expectations or limitations are (i.e., *my must-haves or can't-haves*)?
   ☐ Yes ☐ No

   If *no*, then why not?

   _____
   _____
   _____
   _____
   _____
   _____
   _____
   _____
   _____
   _____
   _____
   _____
   _____
   _____
   _____
   _____
   _____
   _____
   _____
   _____

9. If I have answered Yes to the previous question (i.e., I establish clear and appropriate personal boundaries in my relationships), then do I maintain the limits that I set *consistently* and effectively?
   ☐ Yes   ☐ No

   If *no*, then why not?

10. If I struggle with maintaining my healthy personal boundaries, then does that mean that I tend to be appeasing or overly conciliatory and compliant (i.e., enabling) in my relationships?
☐ Yes ☐ No

11. If yes, then why? What stops me from reclaiming my individuality in my relationships with other people?

    (For a more in-depth exploration of this subject matter, please refer to Accountability and Empowerment: A Four-Step Strategy for Overcoming Resentment.)

_____
_____
_____
_____
_____
_____
_____
_____
_____
_____
_____
_____
_____
_____
_____
_____
_____
_____

Chapter 6

What keeps us from expressing ourselves?

What keeps us from defending our moral values?

Why do we choose to enable others in our immediate environment?

Have we given up on ourselves or have we given up on them?

"Where you stumble, there lies your treasure."
—*Joseph Campbell*

> *We use avoidance coping because we
> think that we are stuck.
> We are not; we have choices.*

> *Regardless of how respectfully and non-judgmentally
> we express ourselves, there will always be those
> who would resent us for asserting ourselves.*
>
> *The choice is ours: Do we choose to be silenced into
> conformity because we want to be nice or to fit in?
> Or, do we decide to be true to ourselves and others
> because we want to do the right thing?*

> *Believe in yourself and live without fear;
> Just allow the truth that you express
> to come from the compassion in your heart.*
>
> *Believe in others; As human beings,
> no one is a fixed entity.*

Chapter 6

We defend and protect our basic human rights through setting and maintaining healthy personal boundaries in an assertive and appropriate manner.

12. In my interaction with this person, what are my choices? How can I retake my personal power? How can I reclaim my individuality? How can I overcome my feelings of resentment and reach a state of inner peace and equanimity?

> *When withdrawing or cutting someone out of our lives comes from a place of logical reasoning, free will, and virtues of humanity and compassion, then this is a 'choice' that we make. In other words, it is an 'action' that we take.*
>
> *In such a situation, we part in peace and experience lasting inner calmness.*

> *When withdrawing or cutting someone out of our lives comes from a place of resentment, then this is 'not a choice' that we make. In other words, it is a 'reaction' that happens to us.*
>
> *In such a situation, we remain emotionally attached and therefore, we are unlikely to experience lasting inner peace.*

I Feel That I Have Been Wronged

> *When we let go of our feelings of resentment we will see choices.*

Chapter 6

Forgiveness doesn't mean condoning toxic behaviors or sticking by and getting hurt time and time again.

Forgiveness is about letting go of anger and resentment and the urge to punish or control others.

I Feel That I Have Been Wronged

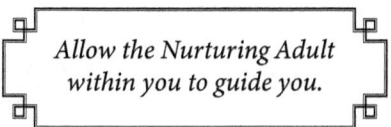

Allow the Nurturing Adult within you to guide you.

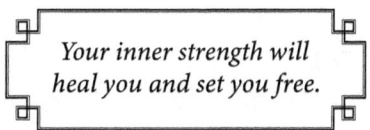

Your inner strength will heal you and set you free.

Chapter 6

Self-Reflection:

Empowering Self-Talks

> *Please pause a moment. Take a slow and deep breath. While reading the following script aloud, let each sentence deep into your conscious awareness. Then, allow the Nurturing Adult within you to guide you.*

Now that I have gained more insight into myself, I make an honest appraisal of my ways of thinking, feeling, and behaving and see my part in my unpleasant emotional experiences without being self-critical or self-deprecating.

Now,

I commit to changing the
internal thoughts and self-talks that
generate my feelings of powerlessness and drive my
conditioned defense mechanism (i.e., my passivity).

To carry out this task,
I cultivate such virtues as compassion,
empathy, free will, candor, and courage that
support self-compassion, self-empathy, and proactivity.

I allow these sound principles to govern
my ways of thinking and serve as a foundation
upon which I build a strong sense of my *Self*.

Now,

The *Nurturing Parent* within me helps me realize that I *am* worthy and deserving of being treated with dignity.

Chapter 6

Now,

The compassion that comes from
the *Nurturing Parent Within* governs my
internal thoughts and self-talks and
empowers me to:

- √ Validate my *Self*;
- √ Stay separate and be in touch with my own feelings, thoughts, needs, and desires;
- √ Be cognizant of my own basic human rights; and,
- √ See that I'm not powerless, helpless, or stuck: I have choices.

Now,

- √ I reclaim my individuality and take an equal posturing in my relationships;

- √ Share my feelings, realities, and thoughts openly, freely, directly, and assertively in a non-reactive manner;

- √ *Establish, define,* and *maintain* a set of healthy personal boundaries in my relationships with others; and,

- √ Protect my physical, verbal, emotional, sexual, spiritual, and material rights in an effective and healthy way.

Now,

I no longer bottle up my feelings, hold onto
resentment, or harbor grievances against others.

Now,

I understand that letting go of my feelings of
resentment is not about accepting other
people's poor treatment of me;

Nor is it about blaming myself for having
such intense emotions as rage, disgust, or hatred.

Rather,

Letting go of anger and resentment is about dealing
with my negative feelings in such a way that
I can emotionally remain detached from those
who have violated my basic human rights;

For it is when I'm emotionally free that I can
stay non-reactive, think clearly, see choices,
and lead a proactive life.

Now,

I let go of my feelings of resentment,
retake my personal power,
and move onward.

Now,

I feel a sense of inner strength and inner calmness.

> *Please stay in the present moment!*

> *Please pause a moment. Take a slow and deep breath. While reading the following script aloud, let each sentence deep into your conscious awareness. Then, allow the Nurturing Adult within you to guide you.*

In sum,

When I am wronged by others, I look inwardly to deal with my feelings of resentment; This is because I understand that I have no control over other people.

When I look inwardly for answers, I become aware of my own faulty patterns of thinking that make me lead a passive life.

Self-accountability doesn't mean that I blame myself; Nor does it mean that I justify or condone other people's poor treatment of me.

Self-accountability is about taking responsibility for the choices that I make (i.e., my inactions).

This is how I regain my control, build a stronger sense of myself, lead a proactive life, and move onward.

> *Please stay in the present moment!*

For achieving emotional healing and forgiving those who have wronged you, refer to: *The Inner Control Is the True Control Workbook: Making Lasting Lifestyle and Behavioral Changes. Inspirational Scripts (2nd Edition, Part V).*

Now,

I let go of my resentment and anger that has stopped me from living a fulfilled life.

Now,

I take back my personal power and control over my life.

Now,

I stop reliving the past.

Now,

I believe in myself and recognize the strength and the wisdom within me.

Now,

I am empowered to move onward.

My Self-Talks

This section is offered for you to craft your own self-talk scripts. It is highly recommended that you design these dialogues in a manner in which you could revisit them during future stressful times—when you feel that you have been wronged and are experiencing a sense of loss of control. Recalling the tools that helped you in the past will enable you to let go of your feelings of resentment and control its downward spiral in a shorter span of time.

My Self-Talks

Chapter 6

Believe in yourself;
Believe in everyone.

Become enlightened by gaining insight;
Enlighten others by expressing yourself.

Your journey together is effecting change together.

Living a Fulfilled Life

To achieve your goals, reach your dreams, and live a fulfilled life, *expand your knowledge, make sound decisions,* and *deal with setbacks* (a natural part of the process).

To expand your knowledge, **read**, don't just listen to podcasts or audiobooks: Reading is an active way of learning; It stimulates the parts of the brain that process visual information and foster creative, critical, and analytical thinking. On the other hand, listening may be a passive way of learning; It stimulates the auditory part of our brain, disrupts our thoughts, and redirects our focus; therefore, it may change or reinforce the way we think and feel about something.

> We gain greater knowledge when we
> maintain our proactivity, creativity and individuality.

To make sound decisions, **reflect and consider all your choices**, don't just react to a trigger or accept whatever you read or hear: The process of reflection takes place in the prefrontal cortex of the brain. This part of our brain regulates our emotions and impulses and helps us make choices that result in better outcomes.

> We make better decisions when we
> stop, think, and act.

To deal with a setback, **look inwardly to find answers and resolve the problem**, don't just blame or focus on other people's part in it: Self-accountability helps us stay in control and see choices, while blaming or focusing on other people's faults makes us feel frustrated and stuck.

"It is far more useful to be aware of a single shortcoming in ourselves than it is to be aware of a thousand shortcomings in someone else. For when the fault is our own, we are in a position to correct it."
—Dalai Lama

> We manage setbacks more effectively when we
> retain our personal power and stay in control of our lives.

Books Published by A. Sehatti

ACCOUNTABILITY AND EMPOWERMENT
A Four-Step Strategy for Overcoming Resentment

BUILDING A STRONG SENSE OF SELF
Embarking on the Journey of Change

THE INNER CONTROL IS THE TRUE CONTROL WORKBOOK, SECOND EDITION
Inspirational Scripts

A WORKBOOK FOR OVERCOMING RESENTMENT
Mindfulness Scripts

A HANDBOOK FOR DEALING WITH SUGAR CRAVINGS AND DEPENDENCY
NCWC's Nutrition 101 Series

NCWC'S NUTRITION 101 WORKBOOK
NCWC's Nutrition 101 Series

21-DAY LOG BOOK FOR ACHIEVING WELLNESS GOALS
NCWC's Nutrition 101 Series

Building a Strong Sense of Self: Embarking on the Journey of Change

Many of us know from experience that maintaining healthy habits is challenging: A minor change in routines caused by a stressful situation can make us slip and return to our old patterns.

Building a Strong Sense of Self: Embarking on the Journey of Change helps us sustain our healthy behavioral and lifestyle changes regardless of the challenges we face.

This transformative book starts us on this journey by inspiring us to search deep within, discover our *Inner Self* (our *True Self*), and love our *Self* unconditionally.

As we go through this process, we come to cultivate a mindset that is rooted in such principles as *free will, logical reasoning, and compassion*. In times of stress, such a constructive mindset will guide our thoughts, drive our behaviors, and help us stick to our lifestyle modifications.

Since we are no longer enslaved to our old habits, we will *maintain* our behavioral changes, achieve our health goals, and experience rewarding outcomes.

This is how embarking on the journey of change will empower us to gain a sense of physical, emotional, and mental well-being (i.e., a state of total wellness).

Building a Strong Sense of Self: Embarking on the Journey of Change has received an unsolicited endorsement from a reputable licensed marriage and family counselor. This book has helped couples and transformed many relationships.

Self-awareness is key to total wellness.

www.ingramcontent.com/pod-product-compliance
Lightning Source LLC
Chambersburg PA
CBHW051435290426
44109CB00016B/1564